Moments of Inspiration

Ruby Mabry

Published by: Best Seller Publishing, LLC

Acknowledgements

The fabric of who I am comes from my Father and Mother. They were leaders of hope, positivity and change, in their community. Your memory is our keepsake. Until we meet again, heaven has our two angels. We Love you, Pop and Mom.

In dedication to Claude and Charite Bissainthe

Appreciation

I knew a young lady who had it all. She had the house, the cars, the boats, etc. Even after having all of this, she complained about everything. The house was over 5000 square feet and she still wanted more. The cars were no longer beneficial to her, because they were last year's model. This young lady lost it all. She became ungrateful, for the opulent life that she was living. Many people are looking for what she had.

As you navigate through life, develop an appreciation for the blessings you already have. Many times, we complain about simple things that we have no control over. Be mindful of what you have, grateful with what you have and you will inherit more.

MORAL OF THE STORY:

Be grateful and thankful, for your many blessings. It could be taken from you, at any time.

Create Your Own Path

Never sacrifice your purpose and take advice from someone who is fearful of their own.

A young woman had dreams to open a business. She was told by friends that she would never be able to accomplish this, because it required hard work. After years of dedication and hard work, the young woman became successful and proved them wrong. Sometimes, you have to push through to get to. Not everyone has your best interest at heart. They want to discourage you and see you failing, because some people are more comfortable with your failure than your success.

MORAL OF THE STORY:

Don't listen to the naysayers. Always be a work in progress. Keep pushing and create your own path. Remember, purpose over popularity.

Wake up and tell yourself;

I AM unique.

I AM special.

I AM powerful.

I AM intelligent.

I AM somebody.

We all should think positively about ourselves, because if you don't think you are worth anything, neither will anyone else.

MORAL OF THE STORY:

When you know your value, you never compromise to meet other people's low standards. Stay true to yourself and just because you do things differently, doesn't make it wrong. Doing things out of the box or unconventionally can change things significantly in your life. It is okay, to be different.

#

Never put limits, on how far you can go.

She was shy and withdrawn.

She never liked to communicate, in front of a crowd.

She never wanted to stand out.

She was never a writer.

She always focused and cared for everyone, but herself.

She is now a successful entrepreneur, published writer, inventor and life coach.

MORAL OF THE STORY:

Create your own reality and don't let anyone control your life or your income. Always believe in yourself. Give yourself everything you want and deserve out of life. You only get one shot.

Know Better

Sometimes, the reason we don't have more than we do is because we mishandled what we already had. Let's face it, when you know better, you do better.

Be faithful with a little, so you can be trusted with a lot.

MORAL OF THE STORY:

You have to use wisdom, as you elevate. As new doors and opportunities present themselves, you have to know how to maintain and handle what is available.

Growth

Growth is a decision. You either make some moves, or wait for life to make it for you. Growth requires focus and you have to move forward, even if you take baby steps. Remember, you are not going through this in vain. The process allows room for self-growth. If you are not growing, you are dying. Keep your head up and continue to grow. True personal growth and development starts with making the decision that one of the most important things you can do in life is to constantly improve, get better, and become a better version of your former self. And, then, it's about committing that you'll work every day on doing that.

MORAL OF THE STORY:

Growth does not happen overnight. It takes time to develop. Learn from your mistakes, stop making excuses and become what you believe. Start small, but dream BIG. Plan, prepare and continually grow through life's journey.

Change

Each day is a day to change your life. Life is a gift. Prepare for what you prayed for. Don't waste this day being mediocre. Let your light shine. You have to expand your mind, in order to embrace change. You can't change anyone, they have to want to change themselves. When there have been habits, comfort zones and familiarity involved, it takes discipline to actually change.

MORAL OF THE STORY:

Change is not easy, but if you want to see new results you have to be willing to shift your life. You have to move in a new direction. If you keep doing the same old thing, there will never be change.

If you want to be happy, focus on becoming a better you. Happiness is determined by you and only you. Happiness comes from the heart. Don't waste time on things that don't make you smile, from within. You have to make up your mind that no one else is responsible for your happiness. The only one that can bring happiness and joy is God. People can never be responsible for your happiness, because they will disappoint you every time.

MORAL OF THE STORY:

The only way to go is to water your own grass.
You have to be accountable for your
environment, mood, mind and heart.

Winning and Losing

Mindset can be the difference between winning and losing. There is the old adage that you can see the glass half full or half empty. You have to adopt a winning attitude and believe in yourself and vision. If you don't you will set yourself up for a loss every time. You have to have the confidence necessary to take ownership of your purpose and make decisions that cause you to win.

MORAL OF THE STORY:

Winning is determined by your effort and ability to believe in yourself.

Value Yourself

Stop pouring out your everything to someone who doesn't even value themselves. If they don't value their life, they will not value yours. Self-love is so imperative. You have to know your worth, because if you don't someone will be waiting to take advantage of that fact. You are too valuable to be treated like an option.

MORAL OF THE STORY:

You are a priority to God. He says you are fearfully and wonderfully made. You are created in His image. There is no price that can be paid to meet your value.

Never Give Up

Give yourself permission to keep going, even when life tells you to give up. Sometimes, it is just about taking baby steps and remaining effective, in the challenging times.

Seeing your accomplishments, in the midst of adversity, will strengthen your faith to finish the work.

MORAL OF THE STORY:

Stay the course and complete what you started! Most of the time, we want to give up when we are close to finishing. Don't let go and see the results you desire.

Inspire

Everyone is fighting an untold battle. Be an inspiration today. Someone is waiting for you to push them through. Inspiration can come from your smile, actions or testimony. Just because you take time to stop and encourage someone, may be the reason that they become inspired. Oftentimes, people lose their fire and zeal to create their vision. Inspiration can spark their spirit and cause their creativity to come alive.

MORAL OF THE STORY:

Someone's breakthrough is in your story. Be an inspiration today and share your story. You are more needed than you give yourself credit for. Open your mouth and release the words that will permanently shift someone's life.

Mental Preparation

Mental preparation is necessary, whenever you seek growth or advancement. Visualize where you want to be, in the future, and work hard until you get there. Mindset is what separates the mature from the immature. You can never go wrong when your mind is focused. Set your goals and accomplish them. Continue to have the mindset of a champion and remember if you think you can, then YOU CAN.

MORAL OF THE STORY:

Change your mindset, by allowing yourself to experience life in a new way. You are responsible for the shift that will take place in your mind. You have to allow yourself some space to be accountable for the place of mental maturity.

Accept Yourself

Accept yourself, as you are. You don't need validation from anybody. Validate yourself.

Even if no one believes in you, believe in yourself. You are more courageous and stronger than you think you are. If you don't start loving you, you cannot fully love someone else. Look deep within and find your true purpose. You will not only inspire yourself, but others.

MORAL OF THE STORY:

Accept yourself. You are wonderfully made. You are a priceless jewel and you are amazing, just as you are.

Practice

Remember, that you become what you practice most. Study your craft, learn it and master it. You have to constantly improve yourself, in order to move forward in anything that you do. Sometimes, because of the demands of life, we set our vision and dreams aside. There is a way to upgrade, even when it seems challenging. You simply take baby steps.

MORAL OF THE STORY:

Practice makes perfect. You have to maintain responsibility, for your dream.

Pain

No pain comes without purpose. Keep moving forward, but never forget the lesson it taught you. These are called growing pains. You have to let it go. Most everyone on the planet, at some time, will experience a painful situation. You will overcome this and this will make you stronger than ever.

MORAL OF THE STORY:

Keep moving. You still have to be present and pursue your purpose, in the midst of your pain.

Transformation

We often doubt ourselves and we lose faith. Transform your problems and challenges into great opportunities. Ignore the negative people, places, things, thoughts and habits. Begin to see the POSSIBLE, instead of the IMPOSSIBLE, and you will see the transformation. Believe you can and you will. Transformation requires dedication and willingness to change. You can never force transformation on someone. They have to make a conscious choice to turn things around for the better.

MORAL OF THE STORY:

Transformation has to be an inside job. It has to take place in your mind, heart and spirit. Once you believe you can change or transform, then you will begin to see results.

Even when your strength is tested, don't let them steal your joy. When you have genuine joy, no one can take it away. True joy comes from God. Sometimes, we let people affect our attitudes and lives. We let them disturb our happiness and peace. You have to make up your mind that no one will be able to upset your spirit and disrupt your heart and take your joy, anymore.

MORAL OF THE STORY:

When you purpose that you will maintain your God-given joy, nothing can make you give it up.

Competition

Life is not a competition. Stop competing. Do what makes you happy and continue to grow. There is only one unique, dynamic and special YOU. Surround yourself with people of vision and of purpose. Then and only then, can you reach your destiny.

MORAL OF THE STORY:

Your competition is YOU. Stop holding yourself back.

Friendship

Friendship is sacred. Never take your friend for granted. Be the friend you wish you had. It's not often you find a true friend. A friend will be there, when your partner won't. Respect it, appreciate it and cherish it.

MORAL OF THE STORY:

True friendships are hard to come by, value it.

Some of you are giving people too much power in your life. When you stop looking for acceptance in others, then and only then, can you begin to advance in your dreams, your vision, and your truth. Give yourself permission to excel in life.

MORAL OF THE STORY:

Get your power back. You have to understand the power and authority that you have. You are the one that can set up your own atmosphere. Don't underestimate the power that you do have!

Wounded Heart

Be careful with who you share your heart with. Not everyone will handle it with care. Pay attention to their actions and listen to their words. Don't take risks with your heart, because a wounded heart can last a lifetime. Sometimes, we use our heart to make decisions, instead of thinking things through. The heart can be deceiving and cause us to lose discernment. Above everything, guard your heart.

MORAL OF THE STORY:

Your heart is a precious commodity. It can't be opened and given to everyone. Protect it and keep your peace.

Dreaming

Never stop dreaming. Dreams give you something to hope for, live for and push for. Dreamers are believers and always strive for more. Eventually, those dreams become reality. Continue dreaming, until you no longer have to close your eyes to see it. Whatever you have thought of doing and have a dream to see it manifest, just know that it is possible!

MORAL OF THE STORY:

Dreams do come true. Once you put your mind to it, there is nothing that you can't do.

Thankful

When you wake up in the morning, do you wake up with a mentality of happiness or a defeated mentality? If it's the latter, then you already have lost the day's battle. With so much judgement, gossip, jealousy and stereotypes in our society today, you must have a mentality of strength and happiness. Let your attitude be an attitude of gratitude, when you rise every day. Many don't get the chance to see another day and you get to celebrate, no matter how small, the joys of life. Be grateful.

MORAL OF THE STORY:

Be thankful and grateful.

If you want to be noticed, choose to be different. It's easy to follow the crowd. It takes a unique person to create their own reality, success and destiny without the pressures from society. When you stand out, what is specifically for you can find you. You were created to be unique and there is no one like you, on the earth. So, embrace you and allow your difference to work for you.

MORAL OF THE STORY:

Choose to be different. The world has enough copy cats.

Integrity

Your name is all you have. Don't taint it, by not keeping your word. Everything you do, do it with integrity. It takes time to build a reputation and only seconds to cause destruction. Don't let your actions and behavior mess around with your character.

MORAL OF THE STORY:

Your actions can cost you.

#

In everything that you do, know that it can be taken away from you at any given moment. Take a chance and develop your full potential. We are not meant to live an average life. Live your life to the fullest, with no regrets. If you never take a chance, you may never know what could be.

MORAL OF THE STORY:

Be willing to take a risk, it can change your life. Sometimes, you only get one chance.

Feed your mind, with positivity. Stay clear of people who bring you down and don't lift you higher. Don't minimize your talents, to please others. Chase your dreams and shine your light, so the world can see. You have to keep a positive outlook on life. It is your responsibility to never feed into negativity.

MORAL OF THE STORY:

Rise above every negative thought, comment and feeling. Keep yourself in a positive space and adopt that mindset.

Never underestimate what He has in store for you. As the saying states, "Patience is a virtue." Sometimes, you have to wait to see how things will work out. If we rush it, it can get messed up. Take your time and let the correct process take place.

MORAL OF THE STORY:

Don't expect microwave blessings. Everything takes time and patience.

Breakthrough

Break through the barriers that hold you back. Let your presence be seen, felt and heard. Breakthrough means that you have made up your mind to step across the line that has been a barrier to your destiny. It is up to you to make the effort to walk into your victory.

MORAL OF THE STORY:

Step out of your comfort zone and start to live again.

Deactivate

Deactivate the negative people in your life. You have to unplug and deactivate from anything that drains you and brings you beneath your purpose. Stop giving attention to things that do not propel you forward.

MORAL OF THE STORY:

When something is not bettering your life, you need to remove it, deactivate it and declutter. Keep your atmosphere conducive for growth.

Speak with doubt, watch it fail. Speak with confidence, watch it grow. Confidence means believing in yourself. It is never arrogant, but it exudes value and worth. It states that you believe it will work and succeed.

MORAL OF THE STORY:

For growth to occur, you have to step out of your comfort zone and become more confident. If you don't believe in you, no one else will.

Have Your Own

When no one has your back, have your own. Sometimes, you have to go alone and have things in order for yourself. Counting on people can be so disappointing, so learn how to celebrate and move forward by yourself.

MORAL OF THE STORY:

Step up to the plate, for you. Who knows you better than yourself?

Share your many gifts, with the world. We have so many unique gifts that can work for us. Sometimes, because of rejection, we are afraid to use them or show anyone that we are gifted. What gifts do you possess? How can you use them now, to change your or someone else's life?

MORAL OF THE STORY:

We all have so many gifts, why hide them? Your gift could be the one thing that shifts your whole life.

Every failure, every disappointment and every hurt has turned you into the person you are today. Everyone will have to face challenges. Some will be small and some great. You have to persevere through the challenges that are sent to distract you.

MORAL OF THE STORY:

Be grateful, for life's many challenges.
You overcame them. Keep shining.

Don't Count Me Out

As long as I'm still breathing, don't count me out. There is never any reason to quit. You have to maintain your strength and move forward, no matter how you feel and what it looks like.

MORAL OF THE STORY:

Never let them see you sweat. Shoot for the stars.

Invisible

When you feel invisible, make yourself seen. Oftentimes, we want people's validation and when it doesn't happen, we feel like we are invisible. You have to have enough confidence in yourself, to see you when it seems no one else does.

MORAL OF THE STORY:

Step up! You have what it takes.

New Season

You can't get to your next season, by only helping yourself. Help and support others and your blessings will unfold. A new season consists of you being proactive and moving forward. When a new season enters your life, you have to let go of the former things. You can't take old stuff into your new territory and season.

MORAL OF THE STORY:

Be a team player. You can only excel, when you do this. You have to remember that it is not all about you.

Procrastination

Procrastination won't lead you to your destiny. It will stunt your growth and kill any potential you have. When you procrastinate, it can cost you everything. You have to make up your mind that you will operate, in a timely fashion. You will be more effective.

MORAL OF THE STORY:

The early bird always catches the worm. The more prepared you are, the better results you will have.

Refuse to be average. No one said you had to be. Sometimes, all you need to do is SHOW UP. Always believe, in the beauty of your dreams. Step out and let your light shine today and every day. You are much more than basic and never settle for anyone who puts you in the average category.

MORAL OF THE STORY:

You are created to be amazing. Don't fall below the standard that God created you to live in.

Comparison

Stop comparing yourself, to other people. You are uniquely and wonderfully made. God anoints us all, in different ways. Comparison will rob you. You can't be identified, by someone else's DNA. So, stop trying to compare and compete with others, when you have your own identity.

MORAL OF THE STORY:

Don't allow yourself to go through any more identity crises. Begin to understand the fullness of who you are. You will, then, understand your value.

Miracles

Miracles happen every day, so never stop believing. Have faith. Stop carrying other people's load and carry your own. Their burden is not yours. Too often, we try to take on their problems and hinder ourselves in the process. Be a blessing, but be careful not to PULL the person you should be PUSHING. God is in the business of releasing the miracles that we need. Take a moment to reflect on what you are expecting and know that it is on the way.

MORAL OF THE STORY:

Stand in great anticipation of the release of your miracle. You have to believe it is totally possible.

Don't Look Back

Sometimes, you must remember where you came from to see where you are going. Don't look back. You have come too far. If you are going to move forward and maintain your new position, you have to keep looking forward. If you keep reminiscing or going down memory lane, you may find yourself stuck in a place that is unhealthy and stagnated. You can't afford to be stationary, when you are supposed to be moving in a new direction.

MORAL OF THE STORY:

Don't look back. Continue moving forward. Even if you have to take baby steps, keep walking and taking new ground.

Small Minds

Stop allowing small minds to keep you from your big dreams. You've waited long enough. Envision, commit and deliver. Small minded people will never be able to see and understand your dream and vision. You have to make up your mind that no matter what, you will live outside of the limited mentality of people who don't believe you can achieve it.

MORAL OF THE STORY:

Take action! Believe bigger than the people around you. Small minds will always try to box you in. Don't let them.

Put in the Work

If you didn't put in the work, don't expect the harvest. You have to keep your hand on the plow and don't look back. When you expect to see results, you have to invest your time and effort. It requires you to give of yourself. If you exert no effort, there will not be tangible manifestation. You are responsible to do your part.

MORAL OF THE STORY:

You only reap what you sow. You are responsible for your vision and if you don't take care of it, no one else will.

Surrender

Surrender all your fears and be propelled to your destiny! When you surrender, you are giving up the controlling side of you that keeps limiting you. If you keep trying to make it work and nothing is turning around, it is time to reevaluate your position. Let go and let God work things out for you. Surrender is challenging and takes effort, on your part. This is because we are used to doing everything on our own. But, once you let Him start working on your behalf, you will see a huge turnaround.

MORAL OF THE STORY:

Don't be afraid to let go of everything that has held you back. When you surrender, you are telling God that you trust His plans for your life.

You Were Made for More

Step into your moment. You were made for more. Surround yourself with people who believe in your dreams and give yourself permission to be POWERFUL. You were not created to just barely make it. You were put on the earth to excel and prosper. You can live the best life.

MORAL OF THE STORY:

We are all made for more. You have to find your niche' and create your "more." It is waiting on you to show up.

Obstacles

When you don't have obstacles, you don't move. Obstacles are opportunities, in disguise, and push us to our purpose. You gain strength, by hurdling over the barriers and obstacles in front of you.

MORAL OF THE STORY:

Always look to achieve greater.

Live Your Life

Instead of going through life, LIVE IT! You have been given the right to live life abundantly. You don't just want to be "alive." You are allowed to live. If you have been through a traumatic time in life, take a moment to regain your footing and allow yourself to take your life back.

MORAL OF THE STORY:

Live, laugh and Love every day. You are allowed to. Don't limit yourself and be confined to your circumstances.

Shine Bright

Every new day is a day to change your life. Life is a gift. Prepare for what you've prayed for. Don't waste this day being mediocre. Let your light shine. Shine bright like a diamond. You are multi-faceted and have much to offer. Make sure you are embracing the fullness of who you are and be bold.

MORAL OF THE STORY:

Don't let anything dull your brightness. You are too great to dummy down. Be the great version of you that you are created to be!

More Work, Less Flash

Success requires relentless work behind the scenes and less display of self-indulgent behavior. People will see your hard work, through your actions and results. The goal is not to be liked, but to be respected in your industry.

MORAL OF THE STORY:

Your goal is not to be popular, but to have and maintain influence. When you focus on the vision, instead of the accolades, then you will see the results. Sometimes, success is behind closed doors, because not everyone will celebrate your accomplishments.

Failure

Sometimes you fail. It doesn't mean you're a failure. When you fail or it looks like you fail, you have to have enough sense and strength to get up and try again. There is nothing that you can't accomplish. There are many people through history who had to keep trying, before they had any results or success.

MORAL OF THE STORY:

Fail your way to success. You are a winner! Don't give up, after one failed try. Try it again and see what happens.

Second Chance

If you find something that makes you happy, hold on to it. Second chances don't always come. You have to make up your mind that you will take advantage of a second chance, if it is afforded to you. This is only with the fact that it will be worth it for you. Somethings are better off letting go of.

MORAL OF THE STORY:

Be grateful, for what you have. Don't be so selfish that you are careless with what has been entrusted to you. You may never have another opportunity.

The chains are falling. Your breakthrough is here. Remember, when you give God your attention, He will give you His direction. Let every chain and stronghold be broken off of your life. Watch what happens, as you begin to walk in freedom.

MORAL OF THE STORY:

Push towards your destiny and break the cycle of generational curses and issues.

One on One

One on one time can give you all the clarity you need. Sometimes, you just need to take a break, by yourself, to refuel and regroup. You need to take time to rest and reflect.

MORAL OF THE STORY:

Being still, in the moment, will awaken your individuality. It will allow you to organize your thoughts and be re-energized.

You never fully master it. There's always room to grow. Growth can happen, every day. It doesn't matter how high you go or how much wealth you obtain, you still have room to grow.

MORAL OF THE STORY:

Your life gets better, when YOU get better. Keep learning and growing.

Mediocre

Being mediocre is not acceptable. Strive for more. You will never be effective, if you only do things half-way. When people operate in mediocrity, they don't get results. Or, I should say, they won't get good results.

MORAL OF THE STORY:

Always, be a work in progress. Push yourself, to your destiny.

Resistance

The closer you get to the top, the slower things seem to go. Resistance is necessary, to get to your breakthrough. When you are working out, in the gym, resistance is necessary to build muscles. It may not feel good, while you are working on them. But, the results from the resistance are always amazing. Resistance causes growth.

MORAL OF THE STORY:

It's not going to be easy, but it will be worth it. Resistance is necessary, for you to gain strength.

Stay the Course

Don't give up. You owe it to yourself to continue moving forward. Life can throw us some curve balls, but you have to keep your focus. Nothing is impossible and giving up is not an option for you. You cannot afford to go back and start over from the beginning. You have made too much progress.

MORAL OF THE STORY:

Fight for where YOU want to be, in this life. Don't give in, give more! Giving up will only delay your purpose and promise.

Malfunction

Don't let one person's malfunction become your malfunction. Many people can't function without drama and trauma. Most people are used to having issues and stress, but you don't have to embrace this. You are going to walk in victory and there is nothing about God's promise that contains a malfunction.

MORAL OF THE STORY:

Misery loves company. Focus on bettering you. Don't let others that love drama and malfunction invite you into their mess.

Humble

Never let a position or title change who you are as a person. Remember who you are and where you came from. No matter how much you have achieved or how much success you have, never lose your faith in God. Praise Him on your way up, because as fast as you get it, you can lose it. Remain humble.

MORAL OF THE STORY:

No matter how high you elevate or what position you hold, you have to keep a stance of humility. Arrogance is so unattractive.

We all have choices. Some of us choose the easy way and some of us choose the hard way. Either way, you have to work hard at both, whether you are WINNING or FAILING. The idea is to find your true purpose, be consistent and realize you no longer have to dream it, you can become it.

MORAL OF THE STORY:

You are responsible for making the right choices, in life.

There comes a time, in your life, that you must honestly ask yourself, "Is this the direction I want my life to go in?" Complacency is never good, whether in business, life or relationships. Want more, be more and do more. When you have direction, you don't waste time. You can focus on what is important, when you have clarity.

MORAL OF THE STORY:

You have to have direction, in order to get to a specific destination correctly. Don't be haphazard with your life. You are too valuable to not know where you are going.

Company You Keep

Pay attention to the company you keep. Bad company corrupts good morals, as they say. Sometimes, it pulls you further away from your dreams. You are the average of the five closest people to you. Are they doing anything with their lives? Are they causing you to grow? You have to have people around you that are propelling you into destiny.

MORAL OF THE STORY:

Check your connections and make sure they are wanting you to win.

Remembered

When you are no longer here, what is it that you want to be remembered for? This is something to think about. The behavior you exhibit daily is the story you are sharing with the world. Are you making an impact or are you just existing? Life is too short. Why not make it meaningful?

MORAL OF THE STORY:

You are so full of purpose and have so much to offer the world.

Mother

Nothing in this world can take the place of a Mother. She is there for you, when no one else is. She instills great moral values, nurtures you, cooks for you, prays for you and she unconditionally loves you. Embrace her, cherish her, honor her, and spoil her. Never take her for granted and make each day count, so that when the day comes to say goodbye, you will have no regrets. Not a day goes by that you do not cross our minds. We miss you more than words can say. You continue to guide us like a ray of light. You're the Queen of our hearts. Another angel gone too soon. The pain and suffering is over. We miss you, mom.

#

A dad is someone who loves you unconditionally. He is a guide, a provider, a teacher, a mentor, a role model and a disciplinarian. He puts you before he puts himself. He is there for you, even when he disagrees with your decisions. He is the one who takes up for you when mom says no. He is the one who taught you how to drive, about dating and how to carry yourself as a young man or lady.

If you still have a dad, embrace him, learn from his wisdom, show him the love and give him respect and some of your time. A Dad is priceless. He cannot be replaced. For all of you who are blessed to still have your dad around, hug him and love him for as long as you can.

He has sacrificed so much for you. Continue to create memories, because they cannot be recreated.

For those of you who consider yourselves fatherless, hold on to the memories and think about the great times you have shared. He is with you in spirit and he is your guardian angel.

Moments of Inspiration

Made in the USA
San Bernardino, CA
26 May 2017